10.99

Pul... ...ons

Film/Fiction

The Film/Fiction series addresses the developing interface between English and Media studies, in particular the cross-fertilisation of methods and debates applied to analyses of literature, film and popular culture. Not only will this series capitalise upon growing links between departments of English and Media throughout Britain, it will also debate the consequences of the blurring of such disciplinary boundaries.

Editors
Deborah Cartmell – I.Q. Hunter – Heidi Kaye – Imelda Whelehan

Advisory Editor
Tim O'Sullivan

Film/Fiction volume 1

Pulping Fictions

Consuming Culture Across the Literature/Media Divide

Edited by
**Deborah Cartmell, I.Q. Hunter, Heidi Kaye
and Imelda Whelehan**

Pluto Press

LONDON • CHICAGO, IL.

First published 1996 by Pluto Press
345 Archway Road, London N6 5AA
and 1436 West Randolph,
Chicago, Illinois 60607, USA

British Library Cataloguing in Publication Data
A catalogue record for this book is available from the British
Library

ISBN 0 7453 1071 9 hbk

Library of Congress Cataloging in Publication Data
Pulping fictions: consuming culture across the English-media
    divide/edited by Deborah Cartmell ... [et al.].
        160p. 22cm. — (Film/fiction: v. 1)
        Includes bibliographical references and index.
        ISBN 0–7453–1071–0 (hbk.)
        1. Motion pictures and literature. I. Cartmell, Deborah.
    II. Series.
    PN1995.3.P85   1996
    791.43—dc20   95–52785
                                                              CIP

Printing history
03 02 01 00 99 98 97 96 8 7 6 5 4 3 2 1

Designed and produced for Pluto Press by
Chase Production Services, Chipping Norton, OX7 5QR
Typeset from disk by Stanford DTP Services, Milton Keynes
Printed in the EC by J.W. Arrowsmith, Bristol

Contents

Introduction – Pulping Fictions: Consuming Culture Across the Literature/Media Divide

Imelda Whelehan and Deborah Cartmell

'Pulp fiction' suggests trash and transitoriness: magazines and paperbacks, produced from poor-quality wood-pulp whose contents are formulaic and sensationalist. These fictions are designed for mass circulation and rapid turnover; they have a built-in obsolescence and will rapidly be 'pulped'. Quentin Tarantino offers us a dictionary definition of 'pulp fiction' in the epigraph to his movie of the same name, inviting us to consider the written word 'fiction' – along with its demise, 'pulp'. The title puts in a nutshell what can be perceived as popular cinema's threat to more 'worthy academic pursuits' (that is, the ultimate destruction of the book by the film). Similarly, horrified defenders of traditional English studies lament the fated take-over by media studies of English, with courses in *Star Trek* and *Batman* replacing those in Milton and Shakespeare.[1] There is no doubt that media studies will continue to seduce students away from more traditional subject areas (in Britain in 1995 there were approximately 1500 fewer English 'A'-level students than in the previous year, while media students increased by roughly the same number). English departments, with an eye to economic and academic survival, are increasingly joining up with media studies. In the light of current changes in the English curriculum, the volumes published in the *Film/Fiction* series aim to interrogate the interface between English and media studies by unashamedly admitting to and taking full advantage of consumer demand, and thereby examining the construction and consumption of the reader/viewer.[2]

1

Tarantino's dictionary definition tantalises us with the suggestion that popular cinema offers the viewer a similar range of sensations to that of mass market fiction. The marketing of such fiction capitalises on the growing consumer culture of the latter half of the twentieth century. Unlike highbrow fiction, which has tended to obscure the mechanisms of production which facilitate the journey of the great work from writer to reader, trash fiction monitors the tastes, identities and aspirations of its audience. In pulp fiction, the author is subordinated to genre. Yet Tarantino reasserts his authorship as a cult director, acclaimed as the postmodern *auteur* of increasingly self-reflexive and highly sophisticated intertextual cinema. In an ironic reversal of the conventional fiction to film adaptation, Tarantino's film scripts are becoming fictional classics – *Pulp Fiction* has become the bestselling film script ever. Far from being disposable moments on the postmodern screen, Tarantino's words are recited, repeated and committed to memory.[3]

Tarantino's work illustrates the changing relationships between production and consumption in the postmodern moment, where the high/lowbrow divide is increasingly destabilised. This volume of *Film/Fiction* debates the multitudinous ways in which such destabilisations are achieved, and ponders their implications for cultural studies today. In particular it looks at adaptations, whether they be the transformation of narrative from one textual site to another, or the translation of history and notions of the past into film. Despite the fact that the high/lowbrow divide is constantly collapsed in postmodern theory and in contemporary popular cultural practice, there is still a tendency – in both literary and media studies – to privilege the literary or the art-house movie over that which is consumed at a mass level. This cultural elitism is nowhere more apparent than in the adaptation of classic literature into commercial film, where the finished product tends to be judged against the impossible – its closeness to what the writer and/or reader 'had in mind'. To offset this, there is, of course, the 'novelisation', a growing development since the mid-1970s which, in Tarantino's case, retains a clear sense of its cinematic origins in the form of a film script.[4] A focus on film 'adaptations/interpretations' of classic literature allows us to scrutinise some continuing tensions in literary and film analyses, which betray an abiding hostility to mass culture and a reluctance to engage with a wider postmodern field of cultural production, where we 'have to think about thinking'.[5]

John O. Thompson, in the opening essay, tackles the unease with which film and TV adaptations are often greeted. This centres around the comparisons of the 'original' with its adaptation. The film has somehow not only to meet the demands of 'literariness' located in the original but also has to satisfy the economic and ideological requirements of its market. The disingenuous notion that superior adaptations successfully capture what the author 'had in mind' is also cleverly hijacked by *auteur*-directors such as Kenneth Branagh. As Deborah Cartmell and Heidi Kaye show in their respective discussions of Branagh's *Henry V* and *Mary Shelley's Frankenstein*, Branagh claims to restore to texts the authenticity debased in previous cinematic adaptations. Yet the process of re-novelisation (Branagh's screenwriters, for instance, 'novelised' *Mary Shelley's Frankenstein*) exploits the postmodern penchant for intertextuality (life, art, other films). He offers the audience an adaptation which is unashamedly late twentieth-century while ironically pandering to a popular desire that adaptations be faithful to the 'original'. Of course, as John O. Thompson points out, the film adaptation does not simply *concretise* an idea of the literary text, whether it be the idea of the writer, audience or director.

While Thompson uses the two screen versions of *The Vanishing* to allegorically pursue his view of adaptation forestalling the sense of 'loss' of the original, Ken Gelder takes up the notion of 'planning' in his analysis of the evolution of *Interview with the Vampire* on film. Gelder foregrounds the context in which the process of adaptation takes place – the 'field of production' (and the production of the 'field') of author/authority, bestsellers, commercial cinema, Hollywood stars and academics – whilst Bourdieu characterises the literary and artistic field as relatively autonomous from, but still affected by, the field of economic and political profit.[6]

Gelder shows that two contrasting positions for Anne Rice set up a tension within the cultural and economic fields. The film of the novel necessarily displaces the author; she is merely one authority among many *auteurs*. Rice's responses to the adaptation offer a third positioning of the author, shown by Gelder's account of Anne Rice's unanticipated intervention in the adaptation of *Interview with the Vampire*. Rice resists the director Neil Jordan's realisation of the book on screen by overwriting her own authority as the sole creator of the work, and in particular the representations of the chief characters. Rice wishes to assert her original intentions over wider production considerations, and does so by denying her 'proper' place in the restricted realm of the literary. The field of cultural production turns out to offer a number of available positions, a hierarchy of authorities where individuals can or cannot choose to occupy the most appropriate space (e.g. Tom Cruise's refusal to have an opinion about the finished film), or can be appropriated 'out' of the field in a way which emphasises the restrictiveness of the originary field.

Anne Rice's battle over the rights to the film of her novel can be seen in the context of Virginia Woolf's view of the literary text as the hapless victim of the predatory activities of a masculine cinema. Woolf asserts that textual authenticity is at stake, despite her observation that famous novels seem to invite visual realisation. Acknowledging Woolf's concern about possible tensions between narrative comprehension and visual apprehension, Nicola Shaughnessy sees Sally Potter's adaptation of *Orlando* as concerned with the exploitation of textual/cinematic strategies rather than with any faithful reproduction of character. It is a text, she argues, which might be viewed as 'an offspring of its original'.[7]

While Shaughnessy pays tribute to the means by which Sally Potter dramatises gender duality (not only in the representation of Orlando's shifting gender identities, but in the casting of Jimmy Sommerville as gilded angel and Quentin Crisp as Queen), Branagh attempts to redress gender imbalance in his portrayal of motherhood and women's roles in *Mary Shelley's Frankenstein* while, as Heidi Kaye argues, creating a film which entrenches gender difference. The woman-positive elements of Branagh's version depend upon an insertion of Mary Shelley's 'life story' into the narrative, and in this way *Mary Shelley's Frankenstein* becomes Kenneth Branagh's *Mary Shelley's Frankenstein*.

In many ways Branagh's stamp of authority/authenticity on *Mary Shelley's Frankenstein* is prefigured in his screen adaptations of *Henry V* and *Much Ado About Nothing*. He is popularly seen as the director-genius who realises the 'truth' of a text as well as offering an accessible and enjoyable version of an otherwise stodgy classic. As Deborah Cartmell observes, in his adaptation of Shakespeare's *Henry V*, Branagh challenges Laurence Olivier's 1945 version of the same play, while activating relations between 'high' and 'popular' culture in order to attract the widest possible audience to Shakespeare. In the same way that *Mary Shelley's Frankenstein* is very '1990s' in its attempt to flesh out the female roles and, more suspiciously, its typically 'post-feminist' will to appropriate 'feminist' issues for anti-feminist purposes,[8] so Branagh's *Henry V*, with its confusion of anti-imperialist sentiment and nostalgia for a social and cultural stability, offers a Shakespeare for the late 1980s.

The BBC's dramatisation of George Eliot's *Middlemarch* is regarded as similarly a product of its time. Jenny Rice and Carol Saunders explore the consequences of the decision to film *Middlemarch* in Stamford. Just as commercial Hollywood literary tie-ins become the sum of their merchandise, so that it is impossible to determine where production ends and consumption begins, so 'Middlemarch'/Stamford democratises the entry into 'high' culture by offering access to a 'literary place' without demanding acquaintance with the originary text (or even its TV adaptation).

The next three papers in this volume raise issues about adaptation in different contexts, from Angela Carter's own adaptability in becoming her translator from fiction to film, to the transference of the grand narratives of history into theme park youth culture in *Bill & Ted's Excellent Adventure*, to the way Mel Brooks's 'irreverent' *Robin Hood: Men in Tights* ironically offers more fidelity to the folk tradition than the previous screen realisations it parodies. Postmodernism is after all seen to be 'full of jokes',[9] and it is always difficult to know whether the jokes are 'serious' or not. Catherine Neale detects a reluctance on the part of critics to identify contradictions in Angela Carter's work, which is explained in part by the weight and frequency of Carter's own self-reflexive commentaries. It is always possible, however, that the joke is on the critics themselves. Even after her death, Carter exerts her influence over her critical reception, though her integrity is tempered by a cool head for business. This is not so surprising, given Carter's postmodern disregard for generic and disciplinary boundaries, where the writer is critic, teacher, and scriptwriter – although Neale characterises Carter's two film adaptations as 'curiously downbeat hybrids'.[10] Carter's screenplays, Neale argues, bear the weight of their literary origins and, as a result, the images tend to appear archaic and risk being rendered comical.

Carter's adaptations depend upon the viewer's familiarity with her work – the literary text is thus both prerequisite for and superior to the film. Since the late 1980s, however, there has been a host of Hollywood films which depend not so much on a viewer's literary sophistication as their fluency with the gestures, signs and symbols of postmodern popular culture. In a sense, as I.Q. Hunter argues, these 'Dumb White Guy' films, as exemplified by *Bill & Ted's Excellent Adventure*, refer to nothing but their own generic forebears and mainstream popular culture. The jokes demand an encyclopedic familiarity with what would be considered 'debased' forms of knowledge. Bill and Ted, threatened with failing history, remake 'history' by exploiting the narrative possibilities offered by popular cinema and television. They travel through time selecting famous figures from the past to feature in their school pre-sentation. This, in turn, is the basis for a (heavy metal) gig. Rather than Bill and Ted awakening to the pleasures of higher learning, their integration of such disparate characters as Socrates, Joan of Arc, Billy the Kid, Napoleon, Freud, Beethoven and Lincoln into the world of mall and leisure park teases the audience with a view of the contemporary US as an achieved utopia, with Bill and Ted as the future 'great ones'.[11] Bill and Ted, by summoning 'history' to San Dimas 1988, obliterate con-ventional views of progress and conflict, emptying the past of ideology. Their familiarity with history as it is recycled through films enables them to take an untroubled voyage through some great moments in order to appropriate them.

Robin Hood would not, of course, be out of place in Bill and Ted's excursion through (Hollywood) history (in fact the medieval sequence in *Bill & Ted* recalls the Errol Flynn *Adventures of Robin Hood*) and Stephen Knight selects Mel Brooks's *Robin Hood: Men in Tights* (1993) to scrutinise the dubious stamp of authenticity courted by some film versions and pilloried by Brooks. In the hierarchy of 'quality' film adaptations of the Robin Hood folk myth, Brooks's is popularly perceived as one of the trashiest. Its expansive and irreverent comic perspective negates the 'real' Robin Hood story only, as Knight argues, to reveal itself as a natural descendant of the Robin Hood tradition in which comic transgression and parody are central dynamics. In contrast to *Robin Hood: Prince of Thieves* (1991), which attempts to locate itself in an indeterminate authentic historical space, Brooks's version self-consciously exposes its own Hollywood genesis by means of playful metafictionality (when the cast refer to their scripts) and knowing intertextuality. As Knight demonstrates, the film achieves much of its dynamic from comically appropriating key scenes from other Robin Hood classics, eschewing the possibility of a 'serious' adaptation, and simultaneously exposing such attempts as mawkish and moralistic.

Knight is not arguing that Brooks produces the 'authentic' Robin Hood movie; rather that Brooks's version dramatises the tensions at work in the tradition 'so powerful that it encloses, as in any trickster-based genre, its own empowering element of trash and self-trashing'.[12] The comedy of Brooks and that found in *Bill & Ted* couples banality with a bravado which seduces the audience into suspecting that a more serious message might be secreted beneath the playful surface – a tension more apparent in *Pulp Fiction*.

In the final paper of this volume, Peter and Will Brooker foreground what they perceive as Quentin Tarantino's serious mission. Charges against Tarantino as exploiting the banal and vulgar tastes of mass culture are refuted in their reading of *Pulp Fiction*, in which the director is seen to redeem and recast 'the pulp of postmodernism' by embedding in the text narratives of re-invention and re-birth. The film's violent episodes (such as the plunging of the hypodermic needle into Mia Wallace) are by no means gratuitous, but illustrate Tarantino's overriding concern with the possibility of hope and renewal. According to Brooker and Brooker, Tarantino's censorious, high-minded critics are, in fact, provided with a 'worthy message' – the very thing they see as lacking in the productions of 'junk culture'. Conversely the more 'worthy' adaptations of the 'classics', such as those accomplished by Branagh, engender occasional bursts of laughter (how else can we respond when confronted with the vision of a giant scrotum?) in face of their alleged weightiness.

The film/fiction interface invites us to debate such ironies, and to insert them into our bank of contemporary cultural references which, as up-to-the-minute knowing academics and students, should be a heady melange of trash and the traditional. Necessarily, academic attention transforms the popular cultural production into something else, something which might gain value as cultural capital in its brush with scholarly attention. The commodification of the classics offers an interesting reversal of these possibilities, however, where a chain of references, local and immanent to the new adopted form, are generated and infinitely dispersed.

Notes

1. See for instance, Melanie Phillips, 'The videotic age of the Philistine', *Observer*, 13 August 1995, p. 25.
2. See David Morley, 'Theories of consumption in media studies', in David Miller (ed.), *Acknowledging Consumption*, (London: Routledge, 1995).
3. See Chris Petit's review of Tarantino's film script of *Natural Born Killers*, *Guardian*, 28 July 1995.
4. See John Sutherland, *Bestsellers* (London: Routledge and Kegan Paul, 1981), p. 32.
5. Angela McRobbie, *Postmodernism and Popular Culture* (London: Routledge, 1994), p. 8.
6. Pierre Bourdieu, *The Field of Cultural Production: Essays on Art and Literature*, trans. and ed. Randal Johnson (Oxford: Polity Press, 1993), pp. 36–7.
7. See Shaughnessy, this volume.
8. Heidi Kaye, this volume.
9. McRobbie, *Postmodernism and Popular Culture*, p. 3.
10. See Catherine Neale, this volume.
11. Although, as Hunter points out, the view of the future as entirely rock-oriented, with everyone playing air guitar and

adopting identical forms of greeting, might be regarded as rather chilling.

12. See Knight, this volume.

Further Reading

Bazin, Andre, *What Is Cinema?* (Berkeley: University of California Press, 1967).

Bennett, Tony, Graham Martin and Bernard Waites, *Popular Culture: Past and Present* (London: Routledge, 1981).

Bordwell, David, *Narration in the Fiction Film* (London: Routledge, 1986).

Bourdieu, Pierre, *The Field of Cultural Production: Essays on Art and Literature*, trans. and ed. Randal Johnson (Oxford: Polity Press, 1993).

Branagh, Kenneth, *Mary Shelley's Frankenstein: The Classic Tale of Terror Reborn on Film* (London: Ran, 1994).

Donald, James (ed.), *Fantasy and the Cinema* (London: BFI, 1989).

Eco, Umberto, *Travels in Hyperreality* (London: Picador, 1987).

Fukuyama, Francis, *The End of History and the Last Man* (Harmondsworth: Penguin, 1992).

Holderness, Graham, *Shakespeare Recycled: The Making of Historical Drama* (Brighton: Harvester, 1992).

Ingarden, Roman, *The Literary Work of Art*, trans. George G. Grobovicz (Evanston: Northwestern University Press, 1973).

Hirsch, E.D. Jr., *Cultural Literacy: What Every American Needs to Know* (Boston: Houghton Mifflin, 1987).

Kamps, Ivo (ed.), *Shakespeare Left and Right* (London: Routledge, 1991).

Lury, Celia, *Cultural Rights: Technology, Legality, and Personality* (London: Routledge, 1993).

Lyotard, Jean-Francois, *The Inhuman* (Oxford: Polity Press, 1991).

Mast, Gerald, Marshall Cohen and Leo Braudy, (eds), *Film Theory and Criticism: Introductory Readings* (Oxford: Oxford University Press, 1992).

McRobbie, Angela, *Postmodernism and Popular Culture* (London: Routledge, 1994).

Miller, David (ed.), *Acknowledging Consumption* (London: Routledge, 1995).

Postman, Neil, *Amusing Ourselves to Death: Public Discourse in the Age of Show Business* (New York: Viking, 1985).

O'Neill, John, *The Poverty of Postmodernism* (London: Routledge, 1994).

Reynolds, Peter (ed.), *Novel Images: Literature in Performance* (London: Routledge, 1993).

Sage, Lorna (ed.), *Flesh and the Mirror: Essays on the Art of Angela Carter* (London: Virago, 1994).

Said, Edward, *Culture and Imperialism* (London: Chatto & Windus, 1993).

Screen, The Sexual Subject: 'Screen' Reader in Sexuality (London: Routledge, 1992).

Sutherland, John, *Bestsellers* (London: Routledge & Kegan Paul, 1981).

Twitchell, James B., *Carnival Culture: The Trashing of Taste in America* (New York: Columbia University Press, 1992).

Zurbrugg, Nicholas, *The Parameters of Postmodernism* (London: Routledge, 1993).

1

'Vanishing' Worlds: Film Adaptation and the Mystery of the Original

John O. Thompson

The one sure thing about the topic 'literature and film' is that it is not going to go away, however much it may seem like a secondary distraction to the dedicated reader and the dedicated viewer alike. 'Adaptation' has been from its earliest days one of cinema's major activities. Before the cinema, and now concurrently with it, adaptation has been a major activity of the theatre as well; and now there is television. Nor should radio and the *bande dessinée* be left out of account. And what of CD-ROM and 'multi-media'? Something *wants* there to be a flow of narrative and expository material from one form to another.

Despite this, the adaptation phenomenon has always made people uneasy. In fact, there is quite a tangle of grounds for unease, many of them unfashionable but not on that account simply dismissable or without ongoing effects in our spontaneous evaluation of the literature–film relationship. I am thinking of considerations of 'authenticity' (the original is authentic, the adaptation is a simulacrum), of 'fidelity' (the adaptation is a deformation or dilution of the original), of art-form 'specificity' (the literary original, if it is valuable, must unfold its material in terms of distinctive literariness, and this must be lost in a filmed version, while the filmed version itself represents a lost opportunity to develop material of a specifically filmic sort), and of 'massification' (the original must be 'harder', more cognitively demanding, than the adaptation, or the latter would not be the more popular form for a mass audience; but then the easy access to the material must involve deskilling the reader/viewer).

11

These concerns look unfashionable because, to put it quickly and roughly, they are pre-Derridean and pre-postmodern. For my purposes, the name 'Derrida' can here stand for a number of intricate demonstrations by himself and others that 'authenticity' is a deeply problematic concept; and the term 'postmodern' can stand for a number of challenges to the value hierarchisation involved in the modernist claim that painting is best when most painterly, literature when most writerly, and so on. The older positions stand convicted of being both dogmatic and elitist, as well as naive. Indeed, the phenomenon of adaptation looks precisely like a crucial case of what the older positions can't adequately handle.

Of course, you can, and no doubt should on occasion, make particular adverse judgements that parallel the general ones. A particular adaptation can be shown to betray its original, to take on material that doesn't work well in the new medium, or to be by comparison with the original stupid and stupidifying. (I even think, though this would be harder to establish, that some adaptations could be shown to be more simulacral, 'hollower' in some way, than others.) Thus, I happen not to think much of the filmed version of *The Silence of the Lambs*, and some of my arguments for that judgement would no doubt run along the above-mentioned lines. But it is positively to my argumentative advantage to keep such complaints particular to the case at hand rather than to have them cover adaptation generically.

Nevertheless, I do think there is *something* generically eerie about adaptation, and consequently about the film–literature relationship insofar as this is very largely to do with adaptation. My hope in this essay is to make some progress at specifying wherein the eeriness actually lies.

Something wants there to be a flow of narrative and expository material from one form to another: what? One important, truly general answer to this question is: the market. This has always been the case, throughout the history of the cinema within a historical era which is that of the commodity; it is now even more markedly the case, as the logic of the market and of the media commodity shifts into satellite, cable, 'electronic superhighway' mode, with its ever-increasing need for 'product'.

Why should the market favour adaptation? And what does the fact that the market favours adaptation lead us to think about adaptation? What do we think of the market, in this field? I set out these questions only to set them aside for now, because I want to examine *something else* which wants there to be adaptation, something which it is harder to name.

Harriett Hawkins has discussed *Gone With the Wind* in a manner which illuminatingly brings out the will-to-adaptation as a function of readers' desires. She focuses on its producer-*auteur* David O. Selznick's insistence on a certain sort of fidelity in the adaptation:

> Audiences, he felt, understood the conventions of the cinema and were prepared to forgive necessary cuts and omissions, but they did not like gratuitous alterations to familiar scenes and characters. In his productions of *Gone With the Wind* and *Rebecca* ... alike he adamantly vetoed changes to the original characterization and construction on the grounds that no one, not even the author, could be certain why a play or novel had caught the fancy of the public. 'If there are faults in construction', he told the journalist Bosley Crowther, 'it is better to keep them than to try to change them around because no one can certainly pick out the chemicals which contribute to the makings of a classic. And there is always the danger that by tampering you may destroy the essential chemical.'[1]

Would that this modest pragmatism were more widely shared! Hawkins continues:

> From his first reading of *Gone With the Wind*, Selznick realized that, in visual details, dialogue, costuming and characterization, Margaret Mitchell had imagined a great movie. He therefore wanted the film to seem like an exact photographic reproduction of the book, including 'every well-remembered scene' either in 'faithful transcription of the original or in keeping with the spirit of Miss Mitchell's book'.[2]

It is at this point that the detail of what Selznick and Hawkins are saying gets surprising. For what would 'imagining a great movie' be like as a by-product of writing a novel? And, even more puzzlingly, what could 'an exact photographic reproduction of the book' be? If I held up a photograph of a copy of Mitchell's book, I would be presenting you with 'an exact photographic representation of the book', but this is clearly not what is meant! What is to be 'exactly photographed' is what Mitchell has imagined. But how is 'the imagined', ideational as it is by definition, to be photographed (mechanically reproduced, from a material original)?

Hawkins quotes Richard Corliss's review of one of the last decade's quintessential examples of widely disliked adaptation, the Brian De Palma-directed film of Tom Wolfe's *The Bonfire of the Vanities*:

> 'Novel readers are a possessive lot' because they 'have already made their own imaginary film version of the book – cast it, dressed the sets, directed the camera'. In many cases, so have the novelists themselves: De Palma's film flopped because 'Tom Wolfe had already created a great movie in the minds of his readers'.[3]

Have we one or two or 'n' number of 'movies in minds' here: the one created by Margaret Mitchell or Tom Wolfe, simply by writing something to be read; the one(s) created in readers' minds as they read? Is writing already proto-adaptation? Is reading already quasi-adaptation?

Something that wants there to be adaptations is at the least a readerly desire, now quite possibly linked to the writer's desire, to compare his or her 'virtual movie' of the original, prepared (more or less sketchily) during the reading process because we now read as movie-goers or television viewers, to an actual moving image experience. We compare *the* movie to *our* 'movie', which is in our view the author's 'movie' (we readers are such faithful adaptors!), and praise or blame, forgive or condemn, as we see fit.

How should we name or characterise the force which is at work here? The aesthetic phenomenology of Roman Ingarden distinguishes between the literary work of art in itself, 'a very complex structured object', and 'the mode of appearance of the work, the concrete form in which the work itself is apprehended'.[4] One work, many *concretisations*, is how Ingarden puts it.

> The complexity of a total apprehension of a work is such that the experiencing ego has too much to do at once, as it were, and thus cannot give itself equally to all the components ... [T]he literary work is never *fully* grasped in *all* its strata and components but always only partially, always, so to speak, in only a *perspectival foreshortening*.[5]

This perspectival giving of itself by the work is in turn to be distinguished from the *merely* particular, subjective, idiosyncratic experiences had by each reader in reading.

All this quickly gets very philosophically intricate, of course, and it is notable how keen Ingarden, like Husserl before him, is to fend off any 'subjectivist' account of experience in general and aesthetic experience in particular. However, I would argue that 'concretisation' is a useful term for both *Gone With the Wind* as concretely appearing to its readers and for a 'something' that can consequently be filmed, be photographically 'captured' or rendered, in much the same way as physical objects (themselves never experienceable fully and outside of 'perspective', of course) can be photographically captured. Adaptation would then take place because there is a *drive to concretise*, inseparable from the very experience of an 'original', and the adaptation is a way in which a certain materialisation of the concretisation is, or is hoped to be, achieved.

Extending Ingarden's insight beyond the literary, I see no reason not to speak of a comparable distinction between the filmic work of art and its concretisations by individual, more or less attentive, spectators on particular occasions. Indeed, 'fidelity' comparisons are best thought of as comparisons between a concretion in one medium and one in another; this would help to account for why one person's shocking infidelity is another's insignificant variation.[6] If, after you read the novel, a very specific 'vision' of Scarlett O'Hara had been central to your pre-film concretisation of *Gone With the Wind*, you might have found Vivien Leigh 'not right for the part'; but if, to use another Ingarden term, your sense of Scarlett had included a fair amount of 'indeterminacy',[7] it is likely that you would not have found the Leigh casting a problem. Hawkins has some historical data on this:

> [F]emale readers polled by fan magazines did not strongly support any particular star for the part. They saw Scarlett in the mind's eye as described by Margaret Mitchell – green-eyed, dark-haired, with a tiny waist – and otherwise imaginatively and emotionally projected themselves into the role. By contrast, Clark Gable was the public's overwhelming favourite for Rhett.[8]

Hawkins also points out the possibility of determination retrospectively donated from the later concretisation to the earlier:

> [I]f countless admirers of the original novel agreed that green-eyed Vivien Leigh acted just like Scarlett as described by Margaret Mitchell ('She is my Scarlett!' Mitchell is often quoted as saying at the première), innumerable later readers have seen Scarlett O'Hara as looking, dressing and acting just like Leigh did in the film.[9]

A concretisation is an idea (or a set of linked ideas). I want now, as a final bit of conceptual groundwork for this essay's purposes, to contrast concretisations with *plans*, which I take to be equally 'ideational'. I concretise on the basis of semiotic material presented to me by the work of art, which I encounter in the present as a complex object created in the past (or, in the case of improvisation, simultaneously to my reception). I plan in the present to achieve in the future a planned-for outcome.

The role of planning in the achievement of the 'original' work of art varies case by case, project by project (with Edgar Allan Poe a notable, and notably devious, early rhetorical advocate of the ultra-planned work). There is undoubtedly an aesthetic of the unplanned, of the aleatory, of the impossible-to-anticipate, and many of the cinema's most exquisite moments participate in that aesthetic. But planning is *of the essence* of adaptation, if we think of it in Ingardenian terms, because to photograph a concretisation, or more broadly 'what the author has imagined' / 'what the reader has imagined', involves a complicated, resource-hungry deployment of material objects, equipment and performers in order to 'materialise' these ideations. And such deployment is impossible without detailed planning.

'Margaret Mitchell had imagined a great movie.' This sentence is deeply puzzling, which is not to say that it is nonsensical or badly expressed. But it is, at the least, elliptical. An unpacking of it might run something like this: 'Margaret Mitchell, in creating the verbal text *Gone With the Wind*, however she did it (and doing it will have involved mental operations of a diverse sort, including some planning), brought into being a text whose concretisations were to turn out to be photographable to excellent effect.' But concretisations as such are not photographable, so the unpacking must continue: 'whose concretisations could, with further planning, be physically embodied in order to be photographed to excellent effect'.

It is all very well for Corliss's readers of *The Bonfire of the Vanities* to 'have already made their own imaginary film version of the book – cast it, dressed the sets, directed the camera': in being only an *imaginary* film version, the readers not being skilled professionals employed in the industry, the reader's version is not a work of planning, of preparing for the deployment of material resources to a desired end, namely, the achievement of a satisfactory second concretisation. It is, instead, primary concretisation, albeit conducted in a cultural context in which experience of the cinema importantly influences how readers concretise novels.

So much for a theoretical framework; for the remainder of this essay, I propose to explore further concretisation and its relations to planning and to viewing, but in less strictly conceptual terms. The various versions of a Dutch narrative will turn out to render some of these relations in the form of fiction, indeed of horror fiction.

The case of the double filmic adaptation of *The Vanishing*, whereby the same director, George Sluizer, made first a European version and then an American version of Tim Krabbe's short novel *Het Gouden Ei* / *The Golden Egg*, is a piquant one – and no less so for having generated what has been seen as a clear quality distinction: the European *Vanishing* has been well-received, the American *Vanishing* has been deplored. This only confirms a broader stereotype about the European art-house film, whereby we would expect the European *Vanishing* to be more faithful to its original, less commercial, more oblique hence more intelligent (presupposing a more cognitively active audience not needing things to be 'spelt out'), less 'sensational', than the American *Vanishing* – because, to put it bluntly, European film audiences are more cultured than American film audiences. On this account, what wanted *The Golden Egg* to be filmed in Europe was primarily the intrinsic concretisation potential of its own material; while what wanted *The Vanishing* (having thereby come into being perfectly satisfactorily) to be re-made in the US was simply, and stupidifyingly, the market.

My own view is that matters are not that straightforward (or that dull!). I should acknowledge at once that, yes, something has gone seriously askew in the American *Vanishing*, taken as a self-standing text: I can't see how any viewer possessing the cultural capital to view both *Vanishing*s comprehendingly could end up preferring the American one as an aesthetic object. However, you could say the same thing about Milton's *Paradise Regained* relative to *Paradise Lost* while still finding the later poem to be of great interest, not least as a sort of rejoinder to the earlier epic; and I do find in the American *Vanishing* a degree of 'rejoinder' quality, despite the film's overall unachieved feel.

If I am not so completely dismissive as most critics of the later *Vanishing*, I also found myself initially not so straightforwardly persuaded by the earlier version as many critics have been, nor indeed by Krabbe's novel (insofar as I have made contact with it via the English translation by Claire Nicolas White). At least, I felt there to be a puzzle as to what the 'point' of the story is. But it turns out, I think, that what particularly puzzled me about the material has a curious relevance to some of the key issues surrounding adaptation.

Rex Hofman; Raymond Lemorne with his wife Simone (left nameless in the original novel) and daughters Denise and Gabrielle; Saskia Wagter (originally Ehlvest); Lienexe (originally Lieneke): these are the chief inhabitants of the *Vanishing* world.[10] What 'happens' is that Raymond murders Saskia and, some years later (eight, the novel says), murders Rex; in both cases, he commits 'the perfect crime'. Rex and Saskia suffer identical modes of death: each is buried alive.

The point of Saskia's death is that it has no point: Raymond has formed a plan for carrying through a perfect crime, and any ('respectable') woman whom he could lure into his car could have been the victim. To this degree, the death of Rex, as the death of the arbitrary victim's partner, is equally arbitrary, though Rex has also 'brought it upon himself' by carrying on the search for Saskia and then by agreeing to be drugged in order to find out from Raymond what exactly happened.

Now, what is the point of telling us this unpleasant tale? How does it instruct? How does it please? For the jacket note for the British video release of *The Vanishing*, Sluizer wrote:

> One thing that attracted me [to the novel] was that Tim didn't come up with all those standard psychological explanations for the kidnapper's behaviour, such as 'His mother beat him when he was a boy and therefore … ' all of which I think is not interesting – there was nothing of that. Similarly, with my films every person is totally free to think whatever he wants, and interpret them as they [sic] wish. I simply provide a blueprint for audiences – I just give them the possibility to think. I know that I once said that people should be 'disturbed' by *The Vanishing*, but in fact I would like people to reflect on what they see … [Unlike in gory 'films with cut throats',] with *The Vanishing*, it's the mental fear, to do with the fact that you recognise in the people something which you recognise in yourself, and which you don't want to accept.

The horror genre depends on the viewer's delight in being disturbed – a mysterious sort of delight, which for the purposes of this essay we can afford to leave unanalysed. What Sluizer suggests is that the particular disturbing delight on offer here is such as to gain from the lack of 'standard psychological explanation'. I suspect it also gains from other standard features of crime fiction being suppressed, notably any ethical meaning of a straightforward sort attaching to the deaths (the point is not that these innocent deaths are 'redeemed' via the punishment of the killer, nor even – though this might be more arguable – that Saskia's and then Rex's own deaths are somehow Rex's fault).

Delight, here, is globally provided by a cool, 'grown-up' capacity to enjoy narrative from which some of the standard devices for providing enjoyment have been removed. The instruction that can be derived immediately from this delight could be stated thus: do not expect life to be be fair, kind and meaningful; do not expect instruction. And in turn this is, while standard enough as an 'absurdist' message, itself disturbing enough to feed back into the horror delight.

However, this characterisation of the material is so far rather too simply 'subtractive'. It leaves out of account what positive elements of the material fascinate reader and viewer. Positively, the excitement of this material surely depends on the inter-section of two narrative lines whose difference from one another is maximised. Each has its 'core feel'. At the core of the Rex story is the pain of losing someone and not knowing what happened. This is something to which, I take it, we can all relate. At the core of the Raymond story, contrastively, is the pleasure of forming a plan, developing it and carrying it successfully through. And this too is something to which, I take it, we can all relate.

What renders this pain and this pleasure, within the *Vanishing* material, charged more strongly than merely everyday experience is that, on the loss side, the protagonist manages to suffer not once but twice (initial loss and then 'self-loss' in the pursuance of the quest for the lost or for the truth of the loss), while on the planning side, the protagonist plans something very bad and does so as part of a series of *actes gratuits* of an intriguing sort (self-injury, selfless good action, 'selfless' while monstrously selfish evil action).[11] Although I have said that the point is for the two narrative lines to feel wholly distinct, one could suggest a formula for their distinctness which would also capture a certain relatedness: on the one side, utter failure of reparation; on the other side, unqualified success in preparation.

The allegory of adaptation here (and remember, we have at least George Sluizer's permission to read his film as we will: 'every person is totally free to think what he wants') would translate thus: for Saskia and her death, read 'the original and its adaptive betrayal'; for Raymond and his plan, read 'the artist and his or her plan'; for Rex, his loss and his quest, read 'the reader/viewer and his or her curiosity'.

Saskia is, within the world of *The Vanishing*, both real and unplanned. 'Unplanning' hangs as an atmosphere over her and Rex (to the degree that his loss of her registers analogically as a kind of carelessness, powerfully embodied in the film in the scene where Rex's carelessness over petrol causes the car to stop dangerously in the tunnel, even though her vanishing turns out *not* to be the result of anyone's carelessness – quite the contrary). Her difficulty with French in her conversation with Raymond also places her in the unplanned, 'spontaneous/ sloppy' realm.

Once she is gone, Rex wants two 'readerly' things. He *wants her back*, he wants there to 'be' her (again) – just as the reader wants the adaptation to bring back the concretisation which was the reading experience. And he *wants to know what happened*, which is more readerly-in-the-first-instance: the reader always wants to know what happens. If Rex's continuing search for Saskia is registered as obsessive, especially in the light of the material's insistence that 'there are after all other women' (this is the whole point of the Lienexe/Lieneke figure in both film and novel),[12] so is the pre-postmodernist reader's search for the 'authentic' in adaptation. But the fatal attraction for Rex is the second: he *has to know* – and in some detail. (It is made very clear that Raymond lets him know that Saskia is dead before Rex accepts the drugged coffee; it is the investigation into the precise 'how' of that death that he pursues to the end.) Now to say here that Rex represents the reader in this regard does not seem to me very far-fetched. We, the reader/viewer, could have a less unhappy *Vanishing* ending very simply: Rex, faced with the bargain proposed, makes the other decision, and walks away from Raymond, to mourn, pick up his life, try to achieve revenge or justice, etc. How flat! *We* want to know; in a way, we thereby become as 'guilty' of Rex's death, and in much the same way, as he sometimes feels himself to have been of Saskia's, in the 'mind game' he speaks of to Lieneke: 'You can play all kinds of mind games. For instance, I am told that she is alive somewhere and perfectly happy. And I'm given a choice. She goes on living like that, or I get to know everything and she dies. Then I let her die.'[13]

Raymond, on the other hand, wants there to be something in preparation, something that would have the status, even if not 'gone through with', of the perfectly executable. What makes his plan so like that of the writer or of the film-maker in general is, precisely, what makes it in the particular writing and filming of this fiction so gripping. Everyone who admires the film singles out for praise Bernard-Pierre Donnadieu's embodiment of Raymond. It is as if this is both the most 'realised' figure in the novel and the most faithfully and resourcefully re-realised, concretised figure in the film because he is *the figure of realisation itself*: he brilliantly sets up an event, perfectly indifferent to the particular being of the person who will suffer through the event the liquidation of that being. This is scary but it is also, in these calculating times, these 'technological' times in the full Heideggerian sense, 'normal'. She, any she who will yield to the process, is there to hand, waiting to be murdered, as any 'original' is there to hand waiting to be adapted.

In the American version of *The Vanishing*, moment-by-moment details are retained in re-setting the material in the US, but, as Sluizer himself says, 'the events are similar but the soul is different'.[14] The obvious point that has been made about the American *Vanishing* is that it has a 'happy ending'. This is not even straightforwardly true (the Saskia equivalent after all remains dead), and is anyway not the key variation on the original material. What has importantly happened in the American version is that the figure of the new girl in our hero's life (Lienexe/Lieneke turned into Rita Baker, working-class heroine) becomes central: she emerges as a version of a generic figure from the last two decades' horror production who has been named by Carol Clover as the Final Girl,[15] the gutsy female survivor (final in a chain of women victims) of the terror unleashed by/constituting the plot.

The reader-equivalent figure is rescued by someone who has been marginal in earlier versions. The writer/director-equivalent figure is vanquished similarly. Who is this new force, allegorically? Common sense might say that the American *Vanishing* fails simply because a balance maintained in Krabbe's novel and Sluizer's first film had been liquidated in the course of crass commercial script development, and that was that. But the Final Girl solution is not intrinsically so dismissable, whatever the verdict on its successful carrying-through in the event might be.

Rita Baker, Final Girl, effectively says to the person with the plan, 'We've got your number, desist! die!' She effectively says to the 'entombed' reader/viewer: 'Relax, don't get obsessed, pay attention to me the living one rather than to her the dead one. I can handle it. You *know* now, beneath the earth, but I am above the earth *for* you and can rescue you (modestly allowing you a moment later to rescue me).'

I think the Final Girl here is, allegorically, the producer. She has the appropriate fidelity, analogous to the fidelity we saw Selznick speaking for; the appropriate 'can-do' mentality; and, crucially, the appropriate suspicion of the director's *auteur*-y planniness (she has plans of her own!). But if she is producer, shouldn't what all that involves, corporately, in terms of power, itself be registered? Over and above certain particular production miscalculations which the American *Vanishing* was patently a victim of, an allegorical reading would leave this Final Girl's underdog isolation, in the narrative, looking seriously phony. And so indeed, as it happens, it does look.

To retrace some steps here: I have proposed using the material of *The Vanishing* to think about adaptation. *The Vanishing* is a tale of mystery and imagination, to evoke Edgar Allan Poe again, who was himself so fascinated by the theme of premature burial. Adaptation, it would follow if one can 'figure' it by *The Vanishing*, is an affair, perhaps a dark affair, of mystery and imagination. Through the imaginative activity of planning, and all the consequent deployment of the material resources of the adaptive medium, the adaptation puts before the viewer a photographed version of what he or she has imaginatively but 'passively' (not executively) concretised in the reading process. (Of course, 'passivity' is not the right concept here: we need another, possibly Lyotard's 'passibility', the quiet, alert openness to the sensations evoked by the aesthetic object, on the threat to which by the market-technology complex he dubs 'Development', with its obsessive need to plan, he has written so eloquently.)[16] Evidently, this interplay of concretisation and planning is given a particularly grim treatment in the tale of Rex and Raymond: concretisation as loss, planning as demonic. Happier fictions could be used to think about these matters: why not? But horror has its claims as well.

I would expect my casting of Raymond as the planner would carry more immediate conviction than my casting of Saskia as the work and Rex as the reader. Let me conclude with a reflection on concretisation which returns us to the question 'What wants there to be adaptation?', now in an appropriately loss-oriented mode.

Here is a sad thought: there are books which, whether we were to die next week or fifty years from now, we will never get around to re-reading. We have, in enjoying them, perhaps intensely, already concretised them once or more than once, but what we have of them currently is only the memory of that. They do not strike us as vanished, dead, prematurely buried; they are there on our shelves, awaiting us. Still, death will come before we take up the chance to re-concretise them. (The situation regarding films used to be even more contingent, but the above holds word for word for the video collection.)

Something that wants there to be adaptation is this: the adaptation would reassure us, via the logic of photographic 'ontology' that Andre Bazin so notably explored,[17] that a concretisation has been photographed and thus saved from death. The 'successful' adaptation, from this viewpoint, provides us with a new concretion experience close enough to our initial concretion to pass muster as its photograph.

But, alas and of course, the very vehicle of reassurance, subject to the same mortality-based limitation, is no less already lost. There are photographs 'saving' the people and things I have lost which I will not get around to looking at again – so saving nothing, at least for me.[18]

Notes

1. Harriet Hawkins, 'Shared dreams: reproducing *Gone With the Wind*', in Peter Reynolds (ed.), *Novel Images: Literature*

in Performance (London: Routledge, 1993), pp. 122–38; Roland Flamini, *Scarlett, Rhett and a Cast of Thousands: The Filming of 'Gone With the Wind'* (London: Macmillan, 1978), p. 199.

2. Hawkins 'Shared dreams', p. 125, quoting from 'the producer's statement in the souvenir programme issued at the première of the film'.

3. Ibid., p. 124; Richard Corliss in *Time*, 1 April 1991, p. 72.

4. Roman Ingarden, *The Literary Work of Art* (Evanston: Northwestern University Press, 1973) p. 332. This is a translation by George G. Grabowicz of the third German edition of Ingarden's work (1965); the work first appeared as *Das literarische Kunstwerk* in 1931.

5. Ingarden, *The Literary Work of Art*, pp. 333–4 (Ingarden's emphasis).

6. Ingarden's more detailed explanation for the 'partiality' of the concretisation may be of help here. He writes: 'Of the entire manifold of simultaneously experienced (or executed) and interwoven acts and other experiences only a few are effected as central and with full activity by the ego; the rest, though still experienced and effected, are only "coeffected", coexperienced ... Consequently, the parts and strata of the work being read that can be seen clearly are always different; the rest sink into a semi-darkness, a semivagueness, where they only covibrate and cospeak, and, precisely because of this, they colour the totality of the work in a particular manner' (ibid., pp. 333–4).

7. Cf. Ingarden, ibid., pp. 249–50. The English translation of Ingarden often uses the more vivid phrase 'spots of inde-terminacy'. 'If, e.g., a story begins with the sentence: "An old man was sitting at a table," etc., it is clear that the represented "table" is indeed a "table" and not, for example, a "chair"' but whether it is made of wood or iron, is four-legged or three-legged, etc., is left quite unsaid and therefore – this being a purely intentional object – *not determined* ... Thus, in the given object, its qualification is *totally absent*: there is an "empty" spot here, a "spot of indeterminacy". As we have said, such empty spots are

impossible in the case of a real object. At most, the material may, for example, be unknown' (Ingarden's emphasis).

8. Hawkins, 'Shared dreams', p. 126.

9. Ibid. While the photographed Vivien Leigh is a 'real object' and therefore replete with determinations, so to speak, the application of a thoroughgoing 'Leigh visualisation' to the entire reading experience of a long novel strikes me as unlikely to be consistently carried through by a reader; but whether it is or isn't would seem more a question of subjective readerly experience than of Ingardenian concretisation as such.

10. In the American version, respectively: Jeff *Harriman*; Barney Cousins with his wife Helene and (only one) daughter *Denise*; Diane Shaver; Rita Baker. I can find no overlaps in the names save for the bits that I've italicised.

11. Raymond as a youth, sitting on a window-sill, wonders what would happen if he exercised the 'absurd' choice of deliberately falling, and does so. As a family man, he leaps into the water to save a potentially drowning child. Then he plans the crime. It is worth noting that the first two *actes gratuites* are virtually spontaneous; only the third, the crime, moves him into 'planning mode' (and of an exaggerated kind) while the spontaneity, the chance aspect of the choice of the *victim* remains absolute.

12. The crucial difference in the American *Vanishing* is that Rex's ultimate indifference to the representative 'life-goes-on' other women in his life (the novel stresses the plurality of women 'on tap' for the attractive Rex more than the first film does) is transformed into a deeply involved if troubled relationship with a 'successor partner' who both saves him and wins him. This moves the American *Vanishing* into terrain which is not unrelated to that of the Du Maurier and then Selznick/Hitchcock *Rebecca* – another film whose potential as an allegory of adaptation might reward exploration. I should acknowledge here the work of Lucy Richer, a student on the British Film Institute/Birkbeck College, University of London MA in Cinema and Television, whose MA dissertation (1993) on the film adaptations of *Rebecca* and